The Mini Manual of
Humorous
Quotations

First published by Parragon in 2010

Parragon

Queen Street House

4 Queen Street

Bath BA1 1HE, UK

Layout by Stonecastle Graphics Ltd

ISBN 978-1-4075-9359-3

Printed in China

The Mini Manual of
Humorous
Quotations

Bath New York Singapore Hong Kong Cologne Delhi Melbourne

Introduction

It's an odd job, making decent people laugh.
Molière

The Mini Manual of Humorous Quotations is compiled from the reflections of some of the most brilliant minds of the past and present. From the deeply philosophical assertions of Mark Twain, wrapped as they often are in a sweetener of humor, and the acidic but enviable wit of Oscar Wilde, with his outrageous and audacious statements, to the sharply observed social commentary of more modern writers like P.J. O'Rourke, Bill Bryson, and Fran Lebowitz.

There is also a delicious mix of the best of the badinage of Noël Coward, the barbed ripostes of Groucho Marx, the slightly off-the-wall and terribly English humor of P.G. Wodehouse, and the dry repartee of Sir Winston Churchill, to name but a few. All have been left to posterity—what a gift! This is a book to dip into and perhaps from which to steal a few lines to drop into conversation or to use as a deft retort when our own wit fails us. And why not? In the words of Ralph Waldo Emerson: "Next to the originator of a good sentence is the first quoter of it"; and although we won't be the first, we certainly won't be the last.

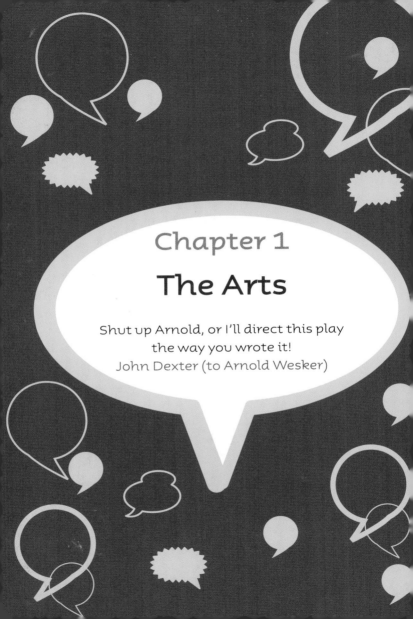

Chapter 1

The Arts

Shut up Arnold, or I'll direct this play
the way you wrote it!
John Dexter (to Arnold Wesker)

With comments and opinions from the great names of the world of music, books, journalism, film, theater, and television, from Louis Armstrong to George Bernard Shaw, the Arts have provided often cutting but endlessly amusing material—at least to those at whom it is not directed.

● ● ● ● ●

Have no fear of perfection—you'll never reach it.
Salvador Dali

● ● ● ● ●

Pavarotti is not vain, but conscious
of being unique.
Peter Ustinov

● ● ● ● ●

Opera is when a guy gets stabbed in the back
and, instead of bleeding, he sings.
Ed Gardner

● ● ● ● ●

One good thing about music, when it hits you,
you feel no pain.
Bob Marley

People are wrong when they say that opera is not what it used to be. It is what it used to be. That is what is wrong with it.
Noël Coward

• • • • •

All music is folk music. I ain't never heard no horse sing a song.
Louis Armstrong

• • • • •

Musical people are so absurdly unreasonable. They always want one to be perfectly dumb at the very moment when one is longing to be absolutely deaf.
Oscar Wilde, *An Ideal Husband*, 1895

• • • • •

I prefer Offenbach to Bach often.
Thomas Beecham

• • • • •

Opera in English is, in the main, just about as sensible as baseball in Italian.
H.L. Mencken

Most rock journalism is people who can't
write interviewing people who can't talk
for people who can't read.
Frank Zappa

•••••

"Classic." A book which people praise and
don't read.
Mark Twain, *Following the Equator*, 1897

•••••

There is a great deal of difference between the
eager man who wants to read a book and the
tired man who wants a book to read.
G.K. Chesterton

•••••

I don't care what is written about me
so long as it isn't true.
Dorothy Parker

•••••

He knew everything about literature
except how to enjoy it.
Joseph Heller, *Catch-22*, 1961

I shall lose no time in reading your book.
Benjamin Disraeli

· · · · ·

Once you've put one of his books down, you
simply can't pick it up again.
Mark Twain (of Henry James)

· · · · ·

When I want to read a novel, I write one.
Benjamin Disraeli

· · · · ·

They couldn't find the artist, so they hung
the picture.
Gerald F. Lieberman

· · · · ·

Would you convey my compliments to the
purist who reads your proofs and tell him or her
that I write in a sort of broken-down patois which
is something like the way a Swiss waiter talks,
and that when I split an infinitive, God damn it,
I split it so it will stay split.
Raymond Chandler (to Edward Weeks)

Never lend books, for no one ever returns them;
the only books I have in my library are books
that other folk have lent me.

Anatole France

· · · · ·

You don't expect me to know what to say about a
play when I don't know who the author is, do you?

George Bernard Shaw

· · · · ·

Critics are to authors what dogs are to lamp-posts.

Jeffrey Robinson

· · · · ·

Here is that marriage of style and content we look
for in all great writing. A shatteringly vulgar and
worthless life captured in shatteringly
vulgar and worthless prose.

Stephen Fry, *Paperweight*, 1992

· · · · ·

What other culture could have produced
someone like Hemingway and not seen the joke?

Gore Vidal

If, with the literate, I am
Impelled to try an epigram,
I never seek to take the credit;
We all assume that Oscar said it.
Dorothy Parker, *A Pig's Eye View
of Literature*, 1937

· · · · ·

An incinerator is a writer's best friend.
Thornton Wilder

· · · · ·

The profession of book-writing makes horse
racing seem like a solid stable business.
John Steinbeck

· · · · ·

To H.G. Wells: It is all very well to be able to write
books, but can you waggle your ears?
J.M. Barrie

· · · · ·

I read the book of Job last night.
I don't think God comes well out of it.
Virginia Woolf (attrib.)

Writing to a magazine that had published his obituary: I've just read that I am dead. Don't forget to delete me from your list of subscribers.
Rudyard Kipling

. . . . .

From the moment I picked your book up until the moment I put it down I could not stop laughing. Someday I hope to read it.
Groucho Marx (to Leo Rosten)

. . . . .

An author who speaks about his own books is almost as bad as a mother who talks about her own children.
Benjamin Disraeli

. . . . .

As to the adjective, when in doubt, strike it out.
Mark Twain, *Pudd'nhead Wilson*, 1894

. . . . .

Autobiography is now as common as adultery and hardly less reprehensible.
John Griff

It was like watching someone organize her own immortality. Every phrase and gesture was studied. Now and again, when she said something a little out of the ordinary, she wrote it down herself in a notebook.
Harold Laski (of Virginia Woolf)

• • • • •

French is the language that turns dirt into romance.
Stephen King

• • • • •

When I grow up, I still want to be a director.
Steven Spielberg

• • • • •

No self-respecting fish would be wrapped in a Murdoch newspaper.
Mike Royko

• • • • •

When asked, "How do you write?" I invariably answer, "one word at a time."
Stephen King

Immature poets imitate; mature poets steal.
T.S. Eliot, *The Sacred Wood*, 1920

• • • • •

A would-be satirist, a hired buffoon,
A monthly scribbler of some low lampoon,
Condemned to drudge, the meanest of the mean,
And furbish falsehoods for a magazine.
Lord Byron

• • • • •

The good ended happily, and the bad unhappily.
That is what fiction means.
Oscar Wilde, *The Importance of Being
Earnest*, 1895

• • • • •

Let alone re-write, he doesn't even re-read.
Clive James, *The Dreaming Swimmer*, 1992

• • • • •

The humor of Dostoyevsky is the humor of a
barloafer who ties a kettle to a dog's tail.
W. Somerset Maugham, *A Writer's
Notebook*, 1949

Being published by the Oxford University Press is rather like being married to a duchess: the honor is almost greater than the pleasure.

G.M. Young

• • • • •

Any time there's a scandal,
we always try and get involved.

Larry Flynt

• • • • •

Nothing induces me to read a novel except when I have to make money by writing about it. I detest them.

Virginia Woolf

• • • • •

If you steal from one author, it's plagiarism; if you steal from many, it's research.

Wilson Mizner

• • • • •

Practically everybody in New York has half a mind to write a book, and does.

Groucho Marx

For years a secret shame destroyed my peace—
I'd not read Eliot, Auden or MacNeice
But then I had a thought that brought me hope—
Neither had Chaucer, Shakespeare, Milton, Pope.
Justin Richardson, *Take Heart*, Illiterates, 1966

• • • • •

I am the kind of writer that people think
other people are reading.
V.S. Naipaul

• • • • •

There are only two styles of portrait painting;
the serious and the smirk.
Charles Dickens, *Nicholas Nickleby*, 1839

• • • • •

It is a symbol of Irish art. The cracked looking-
glass of a servant.
James Joyce, *Ulysses*, 1922

• • • • •

Acting is merely the art of keeping a large
group of people from coughing.
Ralph Richardson

Most people are vain, so I try to ensure that any
author who comes to stay will find at least
one of their books in their room.
The 11th Duke of Devonshire

• • • • •

The play was a great success,
but the audience was a total failure.
Oscar Wilde

• • • • •

This business is dog eat dog and nobody
is gonna eat me.
Sam Goldwyn

• • • • •

Critic's review of the film *Ben-Hur*:
Loved Ben, hated Hur.
Anon

• • • • •

Wet, she was a star—dry she ain't.
Joe Pasternak
(of the swimmer turned actress, Esther Williams

Never let the bastard back into my room
again—unless I need him.
Sam Goldwyn

• • • • •

Shoot a few scenes out of focus.
I want to win the foreign film award.
Billy Wilder (attrib.)

• • • • •

I didn't like the play, but then I saw it under
adverse conditions—the curtain was up.
Groucho Marx (attrib.)

• • • • •

I wanna be just like you ... all I need is
a lobotomy and some tights.
Judd Nelson to Emilio Estevez,
The Breakfast Club, 1985

• • • • •

On being asked how old he was: I am just turning
forty and taking my time about it.
Harold Lloyd

Gary Cooper and Greta Garbo may be the same person. Have you ever seen them together?
Ernst Lubitsch

• • • • •

That poor man. He's completely unspoiled by failure.
Noël Coward

• • • • •

A wide screen just makes a bad film twice as bad.
Sam Goldwyn

• • • • •

The army is always the same. The sun and the moon change, but the army knows no seasons.
John Wayne, *She Wore a Yellow Ribbon*, 1949

• • • • •

It's amazing how many people see you on TV. I did my first television show a month ago, and the next day five million television sets were sold. The people who couldn't sell theirs threw them away.
Bob Hope

I grew up with six brothers. That's how I learned to dance—waiting for the bathroom.
Bob Hope

• • • • •

To find a form that accommodates the mess, that is the task of the artist now.
Samuel Beckett

• • • • •

I have to go now.
I'm having an old friend for dinner.
Anthony Hopkins,
The Silence of the Lambs, 1990

• • • • •

The only question I ever ask any woman is:
What time is your husband coming home?
Paul Newman to Patricia Neal, *Hud*, 1963

• • • • •

Television is simultaneously blamed, often by the same people, for worsening the world and for being powerless to change it.
Clive James, *Glued to the Box*, 1981

You can pick out actors by the glazed look that comes into their eyes when the conversation wanders away from themselves.
Michael Wilding

• • • • •

When asked what he looked for
in a film script: Days off.
Spencer Tracy

• • • • •

Are we having fun yet?
Carol Burnett, *The Four Seasons*, 1981

• • • • •

I am the most spontaneous speaker in the world because every word, every gesture, and every retort has been carefully rehearsed.
George Bernard Shaw

• • • • •

Biography, like big game hunting, is one of the recognized forms of sport, and it is as unfair as only sport can be.
Philip Guedalla, *Supers and Supermen*, 1920

It took me fifteen years to discover I had no talent for writing, but I couldn't give it up because by that time I was too famous.

Robert Benchley

• • • • •

I've read some of your modern free verse and wonder who set it free.

John Barrymore

• • • • •

Someone told me that each equation I included in the book would halve the sales.

Stephen Hawking, *A Brief History of Time*, 1988

• • • • •

Once you've been really bad in a movie, there's a certain kind of fearlessness you develop.

Jack Nicholson

• • • • •

To an actor: My dear boy, forget about the motivation. Just say the lines and don't trip over the furniture.

Noël Coward

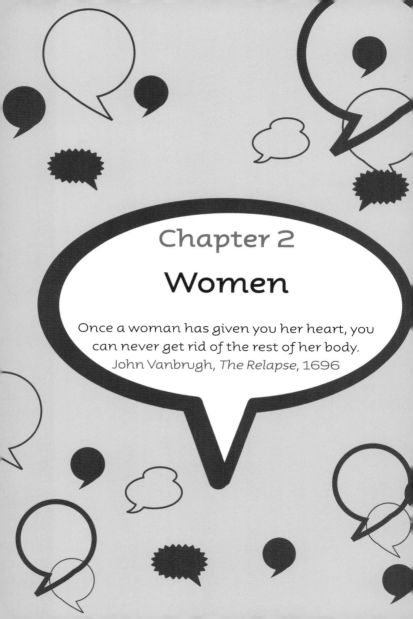

Chapter 2

Women

Once a woman has given you her heart, you can never get rid of the rest of her body.
John Vanbrugh, *The Relapse*, 1696

Too much has been said and recorded about women not to give them their own category; whether women are being funny about themselves or being made fun of, it provides a scintillating ping-pong of insults and counter-insults, invective, and badinage.

• • • • •

Show me a woman who doesn't feel guilt and I'll show you a man.
Erica Jong

• • • • •

A woman without a man is like a fish without a bicycle.
Gloria Steinem (attrib.)

• • • • •

Women's clothes: never wear anything that panics the cat.
P.J. O'Rourke, *Modern Manners*, 1984

• • • • •

It is possible that blondes also prefer gentlemen.
Mamie Van Doren

As long as a woman can look ten years younger
than her own daughter, she is perfectly satisfied.
Oscar Wilde, *The Picture of Dorian Gray*, 1891

• • • • •

The one thing women don't want to find
in their stockings on Christmas morning
is their husband.
Joan Rivers

• • • • •

I don't want to talk grammar,
I want to talk like a lady.
George Bernard Shaw, *Pygmalion*, 1916

• • • • •

Whatever women do, they must do twice as well
as men to be thought half as good.
Luckily, this is not difficult.
Charlotte Whitton

• • • • •

I'm the girl who lost her reputation
and never missed it.
Mae West

If a woman hasn't met the right man by the time she's twenty-four, she may be lucky.
Deborah Kerr

• • • • •

I'd much rather be a woman than a man. Women can cry, they can wear cute clothes, and they are the first to be rescued off of sinking ships.
Gilda Radner

• • • • •

Being a woman is a terribly difficult trade since it consists principally of dealing with men.
Joseph Conrad

• • • • •

A woman's guess is much more accurate than a man's certainty.
Rudyard Kipling

• • • • •

A woman is no sooner ours than we are no longer hers.
Michel de Montaigne

No woman is worth more than a fiver
unless you're in love with her.
Then she's worth all she costs you.
W. Somerset Maugham, *A Writer's
Notebook*, 1949

• • • • •

Plain women he regarded as he did the other
severe facts of life, to be faced with philosophy
and investigated by science.
George Eliot, *Middlemarch*, 1872

• • • • •

A woman can keep one secret—the secret of her age.
Voltaire

• • • • •

When women go wrong, men go right after them.
Mae West, *She Done Him Wrong*, 1933

• • • • •

She does not understand the concept of
Roman numerals. She thought we just
fought World War Eleven.
Joan Rivers

Why does a woman work ten years to change
a man's habits and then complain that
he's not the man she married?
Barbra Streisand

• • • • •

The fickleness of the women I love is only
equalled by the infernal constancy of
the women who love me.
George Bernard Shaw

• • • • •

The body of a young woman is God's greatest
achievement … Of course, He could have built it
to last longer but you can't have everything.
Neil Simon, *Gingerbread Lady*, 1970

• • • • •

The rich man and his daughter are soon parted.
Frank McKinney Hubbard

• • • • •

High heels were invented by a woman who
had been kissed on the forehead.
Christopher Morley

All women become like their mothers. That is their tragedy. No man does. That's his.
Oscar Wilde, *The Importance of Being Earnest*, 1895

• • • • •

I've only slept with the men I've been married to. How many women can make that claim?
Elizabeth Taylor

• • • • •

Her cooking suggested she had attended the Cordon Noir.
Leo Rosten

• • • • •

The trouble with some women is that they get all excited about nothing—and then marry him.
Cher

• • • • •

An archaeologist is the best husband a woman can have: the older she gets, the more interested he is in her.
Agatha Christie

Woman begins by resisting a man's advances
and ends by blocking his retreat.
Oscar Wilde

* * * * *

After forty a woman has to choose between
losing her figure or her face. My advice is to keep
your face, and stay sitting down.
Barbara Cartland

* * * * *

One can find women who have never had one
love affair, but it is rare indeed to find any
who have had only one.
François de La Rochefoucauld

* * * * *

When he is late for dinner and I know he must be
either having an affair or lying dead in the street,
I always hope he's dead.
Judith Viorst

* * * * *

Give a woman an inch and she thinks she's a ruler.
Anon

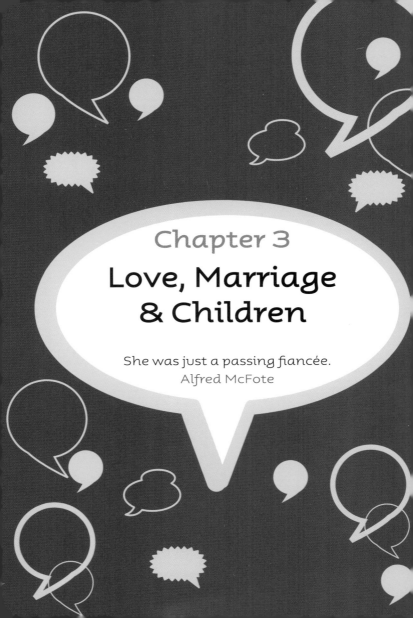

Chapter 3
Love, Marriage & Children

She was just a passing fiancée.
Alfred McFote

Love makes the world go round—love and all its inevitable by-products (marriage, children …) and provides an infinite stock of droll, if sometimes rather cynical, quotations.

. . . . .

Some people ask the secret of our long marriage. We take time to go to a restaurant two times a week. A little candlelight, dinner, soft music, and dancing. She goes Tuesdays, I go Fridays.
Henny Youngman

. . . . .

Marriage is like wine. It is not properly judged until the second glass.
Douglas William Jerrold

. . . . .

To fall in love you have to be in the state of mind for it to take, like a disease.
Nancy Mitford

. . . . .

Love: A temporary insanity curable by marriage.
Ambrose Bierce

We spend the first twelve months of our children's lives teaching them to walk and talk and the next twelve telling them to sit down and shut up.
Phyllis Diller

• • • • • •

Youth is a wonderful thing.
What a crime to waste it on children.
George Bernard Shaw

• • • • • •

Religion has done love a great service
by making it a sin.
Anatole France

• • • • • •

Four be the things I'd been better without:
Love, curiosity, freckles, and doubt.
Dorothy Parker, *Inventory*, 1937

• • • • • •

Where does the family start? It starts with a young man falling in love with a girl—no superior alternative has yet been found.
Winston Churchill (attrib.)

Ah Mozart! He was happily married—but
his wife wasn't.
Victor Borge

• • • • •

The advantage of love at first sight is
that it delays a second sight.
Natalie Clifford Barney

• • • • •

Do you know what it means to come home at
night to a woman who'll give you a little love,
a little affection, a little tenderness? It means
you're in the wrong house, that's what it means.
George Burns

• • • • •

You can't buy love, but you can pay heavily for it.
Henny Youngman

• • • • •

The three most important events of human
life are equally devoid of reason: birth,
marriage, and death.
Austin O'Malley

A man can be happy with any woman as long
as he does not love her.
Oscar Wilde, *The Picture of Dorian Gray*, 1891

• • • • •

Paying alimony is like feeding hay
to a dead horse.
Groucho Marx

• • • • •

If variety is the spice of life, marriage is the big
can of leftover Spam.
Johnny Carson

• • • • •

He's dreadfully married. He's the most married
man I ever saw in my life.
Artemus Ward

• • • • •

Getting divorced just because you don't love
a man is almost as silly as getting married
just because you do.
Zsa Zsa Gabor

Behind every successful man stands
a surprised mother-in-law.
Hubert Humphrey

• • • • •

I've been in love with the same woman for forty-
one years. If my wife finds out, she'll kill me.
Henny Youngman

• • • • •

If love is the answer, could you rephrase
the question?
Lily Tomlin

• • • • •

If we take matrimony at its lowest, we regard it as
a sort of friendship recognized by the police.
Robert Louis Stevenson

• • • • •

If parents would only realize how they bore
their children.
George Bernard Shaw, *Everybody's Political
What's What?*, 1944

Papa loved Mamma
Mamma loved men
Mamma's in the graveyard
Papa's in the pen.
Carl Sandburg

• • • • •

Many a man has fallen in love with a girl in a light
so dim, he would not have chosen a suit by it.
Maurice Chevalier

• • • • •

Love is what happens to a man and woman
who don't know each other.
W. Somerset Maugham

• • • • •

Happiness is having a large, loving, caring,
close-knit family in another city.
George Burns

• • • • •

Bigamy is having one wife too many.
Monogamy is the same.
Oscar Wilde

I'm afraid I was very much the traditionalist.
I went down on one knee and dictated a proposal
which my secretary faxed over straight away.

Stephen Fry

• • • • •

Men have a much better time of it than women;
for one thing they marry later;
for another thing they die earlier.

H.L. Mencken

• • • • •

Insanity is hereditary.
You get it from your children.

Sam Levenson

• • • • •

Love is an irresistible desire to be
irresistibly desired.

Robert Frost

• • • • •

As to marriage or celibacy, let a man take which
course he will. He will be sure to repent.

Socrates

The first half of our life is ruined by our parents
and the second half by our children.
Clarence Darrow

• • • • •

I haven't spoken to my wife in years—I didn't
want to interrupt her.
Rodney Dangerfield

• • • • •

Young men want to be faithful, and are not;
old men want to be faithless, and cannot.
Oscar Wilde, *The Picture of Dorian Gray*, 1891

• • • • •

Marriage is always popular because it
combines the maximum of temptation
with the maximum of opportunity.
George Bernard Shaw

• • • • •

Love is only the dirty trick played on us to
achieve continuation of the species.
W. Somerset Maugham,
A Writer's Notebook, 1949

Marriage is a partnership where no matter how good a husband is, his wife is still the better half.
Anon

• • • • •

Love is like the measles; we all have to go through with it.
Jerome K. Jerome

• • • • •

If you have a child who is seven feet tall, you don't cut off his head or his legs. You buy him a bigger bed and hope he plays basketball.
Robert Altman

• • • • •

Never lend your car to anyone to whom you have given birth.
Erma Bombeck

• • • • •

The four stages of man are infancy, childhood, adolescence, and obsolescence.
Art Linkletter, *A Child's Garden of Misinformation*, 1965

When a man brings his wife flowers for no reason, there's a reason.
Molly McGee

• • • • •

A kiss is a lovely trick designed by nature to stop speech when words become superfluous.
Ingrid Bergman

• • • • •

A poem begins in delight and ends in wisdom; the figure is the same as for love.
Robert Frost

• • • • •

There's nothing wrong with pregnancy. Half the people wouldn't be here today if it wasn't for women being pregnant.
Sarah Kennedy

• • • • •

There is no reciprocity. Men love women, women love children, children love hamsters.
Alice Thomas Ellis

Parents should conduct their arguments in quiet, respectful tones, but in a foreign language. You'd be surprised what an inducement that is to the education of children.

Judith Martin

• • • • •

When my husband comes home, if the kids are still alive, I figure I've done my job.

Roseanne Barr

• • • • •

It is now quite lawful for a Catholic woman to avoid pregnancy by a resort to mathematics, though she is still forbidden to resort to physics or chemistry.

H.L. Mencken

• • • • •

Marrying a man is like buying something you've been admiring for a long time in a shop window. You may love it when you get it home, but it doesn't always go with everything else.

Jean Kerr

I love children, especially when they cry,
for then someone takes them away.
Nancy Mitford

• • • • •

I love life because what more is there.
Anthony Hopkins

• • • • •

A child of one can be taught not to do certain
things such as touch a hot stove, turn on the gas,
pull lamps off the tables by their cords,
or wake Mommy before noon.
Joan Rivers

• • • • •

Never tell a loved one about an infidelity …
Although one dislikes being deceived,
one likes even less to be undeceived.
Ninon de Lenclos

• • • • •

Ask your child what he wants for
dinner only if he's buying.
Fran Lebowitz, *Social Studies*, 1981

My parents were very pleased that I was
in the army. The fact that I hated it
somehow pleased them even more.
Barry Humphries, *More Please*, 1992

• • • • •

Father doesn't hear what Mother says, and
Mother hears what Father does not say.
Anon

• • • • •

Parents are not interested in justice, they're
interested in peace and quiet.
Bill Cosby

• • • • •

I wasn't kissing her, I was just whispering
in her mouth.
Chico Marx

• • • • •

Friendship is like earthenware:
once broken, it can be mended; love is like
a mirror: once broken, that ends it.
Josh Billings

I've been around so long, I knew Doris Day
before she was a virgin.
Groucho Marx

• • • • •

The difficulty with marriage
is that we fall in love with a personality
and must live with a character.
Peter De Vries

• • • • •

Love is not looking in each other's eyes, but
looking together in the same direction.
Antoine de Saint-Exupéry

• • • • •

In Hollywood, all marriages are happy. It's trying
to live together afterwards that causes problems.
Shelley Winters

• • • • •

There are two kinds of women:
those who make a home for a man,
and those who make a man for a home.
Anon

I take my children everywhere, but they always
find their way back home.
Robert Orben

. . . . .

The best way to get most husbands
to do something is to suggest that perhaps
they're too old to do it.
Anne Bancroft

. . . . .

It's not the men in my life that counts, it's the
life in my men.
Mae West

. . . . .

Marriage brings out the animal in some men,
usually the chicken.
Anon

. . . . .

After all is said and done,
it's usually the wife who has said it,
and the husband who has done it.
Anon

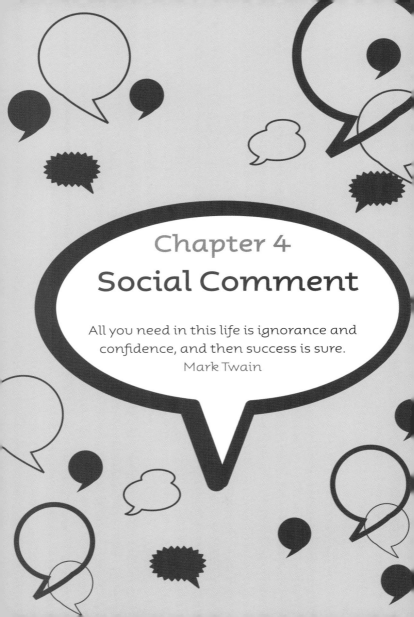

Chapter 4
Social Comment

All you need in this life is ignorance and
confidence, and then success is sure.
Mark Twain

A miscellany of satirical observations on the vagaries of society and its machinations.

. . . . .

Nothing is more irritating than not being invited to a party you wouldn't be seen dead at.
Bill Vaughan

. . . . .

We must believe in luck. For how else can we explain the success of those we don't like.
Jean Cocteau

. . . . .

Lots of people want to ride with you in the limo, but what you want is someone who will take the bus with you when the limo breaks down.
Oprah Winfrey

. . . . .

It is perfectly monstrous the way people go about nowadays saying things against one, behind one's back, that are absolutely and entirely true.
Oscar Wilde

Life is a moderately good play with
a badly written third act.
Truman Capote

• • • • •

There are two times in a man's life when he
should not speculate: when he can't afford it,
and when he can.
Mark Twain

• • • • •

I must decline your invitation owing to a
subsequent invitation.
Oscar Wilde

• • • • •

I was gratified to be able to answer promptly.
I said I don't know.
Mark Twain

• • • • •

The worst part of having success is to try finding
someone who is happy for you.
Bette Midler (attrib.)

People who work sitting down get paid more than people who work standing up.

Ogden Nash

• • • • •

I want nothing to do with any religion concerned with keeping the masses satisfied to live in hunger, filth, and ignorance.

Jawaharlal Nehru

• • • • •

We owe a lot to Thomas Edison—if it wasn't for him, we'd be watching television by candlelight.

Milton Berle

• • • • •

This is a free country, madam. We have a right to share your privacy in a public place.

Peter Ustinov, *Romanoff and Juliet*, 1956

• • • • •

When a person tells you, "I'll think it over and let you know"—you know.

Olin Miller

There are people so addicted to exaggeration that
they can't tell the truth without lying.

Josh Billings

• • • • •

If all economists were laid end to end,
they would not reach a conclusion.

George Bernard Shaw

• • • • •

The right to be heard does not include
the right to be taken seriously.

Hubert Humphrey

• • • • •

That indefatigable and unsavory engine
of pollution, the dog.

John Sparrow

• • • • •

The trouble with the world is that the stupid are
cocksure and the intelligent full of doubt.

Bertrand Russell

All religions are founded on the fear of the many
and the cleverness of the few.
Stendhal

. . . . .

If men are so wicked with religion,
what would they be without it?
Benjamin Franklin

. . . . .

It is difficult to see why lace should be so
expensive; it is mostly holes.
Mary Wilson Little

. . . . .

Any fool can tell the truth, but it requires a man
of some sense to know how to lie well.
Samuel Butler

. . . . .

A lie can be halfway round the world before
the truth has got its boots on.
James Callaghan

I don't like to share my personal life...it wouldn't be personal if I shared it.
George Clooney

• • • • •

How come there's only one Monopolies Commission?
Nigel Rees, *Graffiti 4*, 1982

• • • • •

I don't at all like knowing what people say of me behind my back. It makes one far too conceited.
Oscar Wilde, *An Ideal Husband*, 1895

• • • • •

A successful lawsuit is one worn by a policeman.
Robert Frost

• • • • •

I'll tell you one thing: Don't ever give anybody your best advice, because they're not going to follow it.
Jack Nicholson

Committees are a group of the unfit appointed
by the unwilling to do the unnecessary.
Carl C. Byers

* * * * *

Let's find out what everyone is doing,
And then stop everyone from doing it.
A.P. Herbert

* * * * *

A chrysanthemum by any other name
would be easier to spell.
William J. Johnston

* * * * *

Some cause happiness wherever they go;
others whenever they go.
Oscar Wilde

* * * * *

A jury consists of twelve persons chosen to
decide who has the better lawyer.
Robert Frost

I hate to advocate drugs, alcohol, violence,
or insanity to anyone, but they've
always worked for me.
Hunter S. Thompson

. . . . .

Unseen, in the background, Fate was quietly
slipping the lead into the boxing glove.
P.G. Wodehouse, *Very Good Jeeves*, 1930

. . . . .

We should take care not to make the intellect
our god; it has, of course, powerful muscles,
but no personality.
Albert Einstein

. . . . .

All our final decisions are made in a state of
mind that is not going to last.
Marcel Proust

. . . . .

The physician can bury his mistakes, but the
architect can only advise his client to plant vines.
Frank Lloyd Wright

Critics are like eunuchs in a harem: they know
how it's done, they've seen it done every day, but
they're unable to do it themselves.
Brendan Behan (attrib.)

* * * * *

Honest criticism is hard to take, particularly from a
relative, a friend, an acquaintance, or a stranger.
Franklin P. Jones

* * * * *

Never buy anything simply because
it is expensive.
Oscar Wilde

* * * * *

The price of freedom of religion, or of speech,
or of the press, is that we must put up with
a good deal of rubbish.
Robert Jackson

* * * * *

The most beautiful things in the world are the
most useless—peacocks and lilies, for instance.
John Ruskin

Only the shallow know themselves.
Oscar Wilde

• • • • •

You will always find some Eskimo ready
to instruct the Congolese on how to
cope with heatwaves.
Stanislaw J. Lec

• • • • •

A celebrity is a person who works hard all his life
to become well known, then wears dark glasses
to avoid being recognized.
Fred Allen

• • • • •

Eccentricity, to be socially acceptable, had still
to have at least four or five generations
of inbreeding behind it.
Osbert Lancaster, *All Done From Memory*, 1953

• • • • •

It is better to keep your mouth shut and to appear
stupid than to open it and remove all doubt.
Mark Twain

It usually takes me more than three weeks to prepare a good impromptu speech.
Mark Twain

• • • • •

The word "good" has many meanings. For example, if a man were to shoot his grandmother at a range of five hundred yards, I should call him a good shot, but not necessarily a good man.
G.K. Chesterton

• • • • •

The fellow who laughs last may laugh best, but he gets the reputation of being very slow-witted.
Leo Rosten

• • • • •

It's my rule never to lose me temper till it would be detrimental to keep it.
Sean O'Casey, *The Plough and the Stars*, 1926

• • • • •

Psychiatry enables us to correct our faults by confessing our parents' shortcomings.
Laurence Peter

Income tax has made more liars out of the
American people than golf.
Will Rogers

• • • • •

Good taste is better than bad taste,
but bad taste is better than no taste.
Arnold Bennett

• • • • •

Your friend is the man who knows all about you,
and still likes you.
Elbert Hubbard, *The Notebook*, 1927

• • • • •

He has all the characteristics of a
dog—except loyalty.
Sam Houston

• • • • •

When everyone is somebody,
Then no one's anybody.
W.S. Gilbert, *The Gondoliers*, 1889

How many cares one loses when one decides not
to be something, but to be someone.
Coco Chanel

．．．．．

The opposite of talking isn't listening.
The opposite of talking is waiting.
Fran Lebowitz, *Social Studies*, 1981

．．．．．

It wasn't my finest hour.
It wasn't even my finest half hour.
Bill Clinton

．．．．．

We are masters of the unsaid words, but slaves
of those we let slip out.
Winston Churchill

．．．．．

It's a recession when your neighbor loses his job;
it's a depression when you lose yours.
Harry S. Truman

You must come again when you have less time.
Walter Sickert

• • • • •

An aristocracy in a republic is like a chicken whose head has been cut off: it may run about in a lively way, but in fact it is dead.
Nancy Mitford

• • • • •

Never take a reference from a clergyman. They always want to give someone a second chance.
Lady Selborne

• • • • •

Anyone seen on a bus over the age of thirty has been a failure in life.
Loelia, Duchess of Westminster

• • • • •

He that has a secret to hide should not only hide it but hide that he has it to hide.
Thomas Carlyle

Friends are God's apology for relations.
Hugh Kingsmill

•••••

The one important thing I have learned over the years is the difference between taking one's work seriously and taking one's self seriously. The first is imperative and the second is disastrous.
Margot Fonteyn

•••••

If you obey all the rules, you miss all the fun.
Katharine Hepburn

•••••

Laugh and the world laughs with you.
Snore and you sleep alone.
Anthony Burgess

•••••

Age is deformed, youth unkind,
We scorn their bodies, they our mind.
Thomas Bastard, *Chrestoleros*

What is the difference between a taxidermist
and a tax collector?
The taxidermist takes only your skin.
Mark Twain

• • • • •

Listen. Say less rather than more.
If you want to be smart, play stupid!
Helena Rubinstein

• • • • •

Happiness is nothing more than good health
and a bad memory.
Albert Schweitzer

• • • • •

The trouble with high-tech is that you always
end up using scissors.
David Hockney

• • • • •

Work is the curse of the drinking class.
Oscar Wilde

A little inaccuracy sometimes saves
tons of explanation.
Saki, The Square Egg, 1924

• • • • •

It's true hard work never killed anybody,
but I figure why take the chance?
Ronald Reagan

• • • • •

Long experience has told me that to be criticized
is not always to be wrong.
Anthony Eden

• • • • •

Work expands so as to fill the time available
for its completion.
C. Northcote Parkinson, Parkinson's Law, 1958

• • • • •

Life is a mirror: if you frown at it, it frowns back;
if you smile, it returns the greeting.
William Makepeace Thackeray

Good manners is the art of making those people easy with whom we converse. Whoever makes the fewest people uneasy is the best bred in the company.
Jonathan Swift

* * * * *

Moral indignation is jealousy with a halo.
H.G. Wells

* * * * *

Art is I; science is we.
Claude Bernard

* * * * *

Hindsight is always twenty-twenty.
Billy Wilder

* * * * *

The trouble with being in the rat-race is that even if you win, you're still a rat.
Lily Tomlin

There are two things to aim at in this life: first to get what you want; and, after that, to enjoy it. Only the wisest of mankind achieve the second.

Logan Pearsall Smith

* * * * *

Duty is what one expects from others, it is not what one does oneself.

Oscar Wilde, *A Woman of No Importance*, 1893

* * * * *

If you can keep your head while those about you are losing theirs, perhaps you do not understand the situation.

Nelson Boswell

* * * * *

The world is divided into people who do things and people who get the credit. Try, if you can, to belong to the first class. There's far less competition.

Dwight Morrow

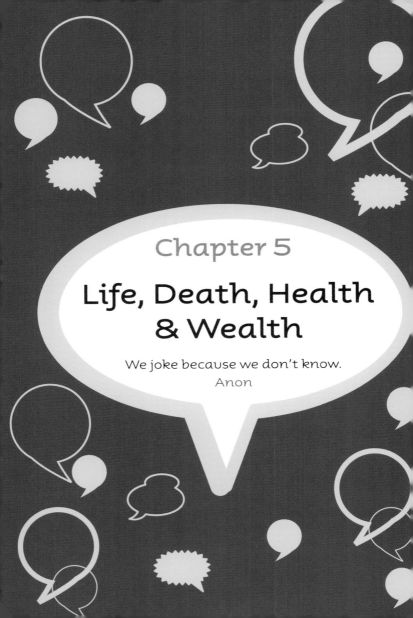

Chapter 5

Life, Death, Health & Wealth

We joke because we don't know.
Anon

Four fundamentals: life, death, health, and wealth, are normally seen as serious subjects, but they give rise to a surprisingly large amount of amusing irreverence.

* * * * *

Life would be infinitely happier if we could only be born at the age of eighty and gradually approach eighteen.
Mark Twain

* * * * *

Whoever said money can't buy happiness didn't know where to shop.
Gittel Hudnick

* * * * *

In the city a funeral is just an interruption of traffic; in the country it is a form of popular entertainment.
George Ade

* * * * *

It's not that I'm afraid to die, I just don't want to be there when it happens.
Woody Allen, *Without Feathers*, 1976

If you take epitaphs seriously, we ought to bury
the living and resurrect the dead.
Mark Twain

• • • • •

Death is the most convenient time
to tax rich people.
David Lloyd George

• • • • •

Retirement means twice as much husband
and half as much money.
Anon

• • • • •

It's a funny old world—a man's lucky
if he gets out of it alive.
W.C. Fields, *You're Telling Me*, 1934

• • • • •

Plan for this world as if you
expect to live forever;
but plan for the hereafter as if
you expect to die tomorrow.
Solomon Ibn Gabirol

Smoking is one of the leading causes of statistics.
Fletcher Knebel

* * * * *

TB or not TB, that is the congestion.
Woody Allen

* * * * *

Hovering between wife and death.
James Montgomery

* * * * *

The meaning of life is that it stops.
Franz Kafka

* * * * *

I don't need you to remind me of my age,
I have a bladder to do that for me.
Stephen Fry, *Paperweight*, 1992

* * * * *

Before undergoing a surgical operation, arrange
your temporal affairs. You may live.
Ambrose Bierce

Youth cannot know how age thinks and feels.
But old men are guilty if they forget what
it was to be young.
J. K. Rowling

• • • • •

He died of cirrhosis of the liver. It costs money
to die of cirrhosis of the liver.
P.G. Wodehouse

• • • • •

You know you're getting old when the candles
cost more than the cake.
Bob Hope

• • • • •

A bank is a place that will lend you money if you
can prove that you don't need it.
Bob Hope

• • • • •

One of the strangest things about life is that the
poor, who need money the most, are the very
ones who never have it.
Finley Dunne

When you don't have any money,
the problem is food.
When you have money, it's sex.
When you have both, it's health.
J.P. Donleavy, *The Ginger Man*, 1955

• • • • •

Our rabbi is so poor that if he didn't fast every
Monday and Thursday, he'd starve to death.
Jewish saying

• • • • •

Saving is a very fine thing. Especially when
your parents have done it for you.
Winston Churchill (attrib.)

• • • • •

Money is better than poverty, if only for
financial reasons.
Woody Allen, *Without Feathers*, 1972

• • • • •

There is nothing more demoralizing than a
small but adequate income.
Edmund Wilson

The two most beautiful words in the English language are "check enclosed."
Dorothy Parker

• • • • •

The trouble with being poor is that it takes up all your time.
Willem de Kooning

• • • • •

I don't want money. It is only people who pay their bills who want that, and I never pay mine.
Oscar Wilde, *The Picture of Dorian Gray*, 1891

• • • • •

Cocaine is God's way of saying you're making too much money.
Robin Williams

• • • • •

I have long been of the opinion that if work were such a splendid thing the rich would have kept more of it for themselves.
Bruce Grocott

The most pleasing thing that money can
buy is privacy.
Calouste Gulbenkian

* * * * *

Why does life keep teaching me lessons I have
no desire to learn?
Ashleigh Brilliant

* * * * *

Whenever I feel the need for exercise I go and lie
down for half an hour until the feeling passes.
Will Rogers

* * * * *

Take care of your body. It's the only place
you have to live.
Jim Rohn

* * * * *

Nobody was ever meant
To remember or invent
What he did with every cent.
Robert Frost

We drink each other's health and spoil our own.
Jerome K. Jerome,
Idle Thoughts of an Idle Fellow, 1886

• • • • •

Money is not the only answer,
but it makes a difference.
Barack Obama

• • • • •

Being young is not having any money; being
young is not minding not having any money.
Katharine Whitehorn, *Observations*, 1970

• • • • •

Real freedom is having nothing.
I was freer when I didn't have a cent.
Mike Tyson

• • • • •

Economy is going without something you
do want in case you should, some day, want
something you probably won't want.
Anthony Hope, *The Dolly Dialogues*, 1894

My doctor is wonderful. Once, when
I couldn't afford an operation,
he touched up the X-rays.
Joey Bishop

• • • • •

The meek shall inherit the earth,
but not the mineral rights.
John Paul Getty

• • • • •

Early to rise and early to bed
Makes a man healthy, wealthy, and dead.
James Thurber

• • • • •

There is no cure for birth or death
save to enjoy the interval.
George Santayana

• • • • •

Fitness—if it came in a bottle, everybody would
have a great body.
Cher

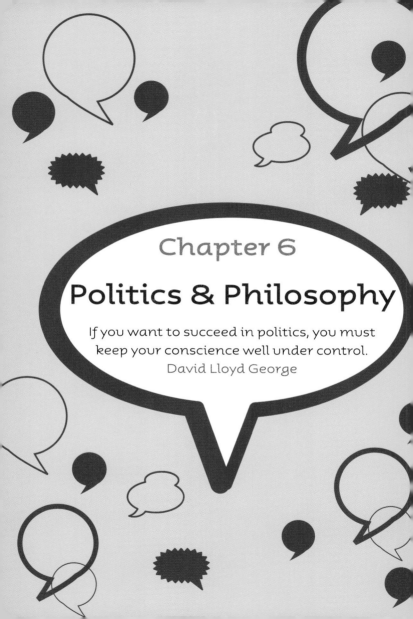

Chapter 6

Politics & Philosophy

If you want to succeed in politics, you must keep your conscience well under control.
David Lloyd George

There are many humorous quotations which are not so much funny as resoundingly true, and rather than generating guffaws of laughter, produce in us a wry smile. As George Bernard Shaw said: "My way of joking is to tell the truth."

* * * * *

Politics—the art of getting votes from the poor and campaign funds from the rich by promising to protect each from the other.
Oscar Ameringer

* * * * *

A serious and good philosophical work could be written consisting entirely of jokes.
Ludwig Wittgenstein

* * * * *

I think I think; therefore I think I am.
Ambrose Bierce

* * * * *

All politics are based on the indifference of the majority.
James Reston

Reagan won because he ran against
Jimmy Carter. Had Reagan run unopposed,
he would have lost.
Mort Sahl

• • • • •

A diplomat is a man who thinks twice
before he says nothing.
Frederick Sawyer

• • • • •

The art of government consists in taking as
much money as possible from one class
of citizen to give to the other.
Voltaire

• • • • •

I think there is something out there watching
over us. Unfortunately, it is the government.
Woody Allen

• • • • •

Politics is perhaps the only profession for which
no preparation is thought necessary.
Robert Louis Stevenson

Too bad all the people who know how
to run the country are busy driving
taxicabs and cutting hair.
George Burns

• • • • •

A Government that robs Peter to pay Paul can,
as a rule, calculate on the support of Paul.
George Bernard Shaw

• • • • •

Democracy is the worst form of government
except for all those other forms that have
been tried from time to time.
Winston Churchill

• • • • •

Politicians are the same all over. They promise to
build a bridge even when there's no river.
Nikita Khrushchev

• • • • •

If I were married to her, I'd be sure to have dinner
ready when she got home.
George Shultz (of Margaret Thatcher)

I'm so overexposed, I'm making
Paris Hilton look like a recluse.
Barack Obama

• • • • •

What's wrong with being a boring kind of guy?
George H. W. Bush

• • • • •

When I was a boy I was told that anyone could
become President. I'm beginning to believe it.
Clarence Darrow

• • • • •

In an autocracy, one person has his way;
in an aristocracy a few people have their way;
in a democracy no one has his way.
Celia Green, *The Decline and Fall of Science*

• • • • •

The inherent vice of capitalism is
the unequal sharing of blessings;
the inherent virtue of socialism is
the equal sharing of miseries.
Winston Churchill

Englishmen never will be slaves;
they are free to do whatever the government
and public opinion allow them to do.
George Bernard Shaw

•••••

A politician is an animal that can sit on a fence
and keep both ears to the ground.
H.L. Mencken

•••••

Man is an animal that makes bargains;
no other animal does this—no dog exchanges
bones with another.
Adam Smith

•••••

You don't tell deliberate lies,
but sometimes you have to be evasive.
Margaret Thatcher

•••••

A politician is a man who approaches
every question with an open mouth.
George Canning

The mistake a lot of politicians make is in forgetting they've been appointed and thinking they've been anointed.
Claude D. Pepper

• • • • •

Reagan was probably the first modern president to treat the post as a part-time job, one way of helping to fill the otherwise blank days of retirement.
Simon Hoggart, *America, 1990*

• • • • •

It is exciting to have a real crisis on your hands, when you have spent half your political life dealing with humdrum issues like the environment.
Margaret Thatcher

• • • • •

Politics is not a bad profession. If you succeed there are many rewards, if you disgrace yourself you can always write a book.
Ronald Reagan

I am on the right wing of the middle of the road
and with a strong radical bias.
Anon

* * * * *

Richard Nixon means never having
to say you're sorry.
Wilfred Sheed

* * * * *

Anarchism is a game at which the police
can beat you.
George Bernard Shaw, *Misalliance*, 1914

* * * * *

Republicans raise dahlias, Dalmatians,
and eyebrows.
Democrats raise Airedales, kids, and taxes.
Will Stanton

* * * * *

Is it progress if a cannibal uses a fork?
Stanislaw J. Lec

It's far easier to forgive an enemy after
you've got even with him.
Olin Miller

• • • • •

Intuition is reason in a hurry.
Holbrook Jackson

• • • • •

The follies which a man regrets most
in his life are those which he didn't
commit when he had the opportunity.
Helen Rowland

• • • • •

The only thing experience teaches us is that
experience teaches us nothing.
André Maurois

• • • • •

The advantage of a bad memory is that
one enjoys several times the same good
things for the first time.
Friedrich Nietzsche

Man is the only animal that blushes—or ought to.
Mark Twain

● ● ● ● ●

If you keep your mouth shut,
you will never put your foot in it.
Austin O'Malley

● ● ● ● ●

Even when all the experts agree,
they may well be mistaken.
Bertrand Russell

● ● ● ● ●

One never dives into the water to
save a drowning man more eagerly
than when there are others present
who dare not take the risk.
Friedrich Nietzsche

● ● ● ● ●

The process of scientific discovery is, in effect,
a continual flight from wonder.
Albert Einstein

It is better to waste one's youth than to
do nothing with it at all.
*Georges Courteline, La Philosophie de
Georges Courteline, 1948*

• • • • •

It is better to have loved and lost
than never to have lost at all.
Samuel Butler

• • • • •

Between us, we cover all knowledge; he knows all
that can be known, and I know the rest.
Mark Twain (of Rudyard Kipling)

• • • • •

Wise men think their thoughts;
fools proclaim them.
Heinrich Heine

• • • • •

We need not worry so much about what man
descends from—it's what he descends to that
shames the human race.
Mark Twain

When dealing with the insane, the best method
is to pretend to be sane.
Herman Hesse

• • • • •

If only we'd stop trying to be happy
we could have a pretty good time.
Edith Wharton

• • • • •

Heresy is only another word for
freedom of thought.
Graham Greene

• • • • •

Few people can be happy unless they hate
some other person, nation, or creed.
Bertrand Russell

• • • • •

We act as though comfort and luxury were
the chief requirements of life, when all we
need to make us really happy is something
to be enthusiastic about.
Charles Kingsley

True equality exists in the treatment of unequal things unequally.
Aristotle

• • • • •

The man who is a pessimist before forty-eight knows too much; the man who is an optimist after forty-eight knows too little.
Mark Twain

• • • • •

Tolerance is only another name for indifference.
W. Somerset Maugham

• • • • •

I think that bad philosophers may have a certain influence, good philosophers, never.
Bertrand Russell

• • • • •

Philosophy is common sense in a dress suit.
Oliver Braston

He has not learned the lesson of life who does
not every day surmount a fear.
Ralph Waldo Emerson

. . . . .

I have a new philosophy: I'm only going to
dread one day at a time.
Charles Schulz

. . . . .

Man prefers to believe what he prefers to be true.
Francis Bacon

. . . . .

Man does not live by words alone, despite the fact
that he sometimes has to eat them.
Adlai Stevenson

. . . . .

Everyone complains of his memory,
no one of his judgment.
François de La Rochefoucauld

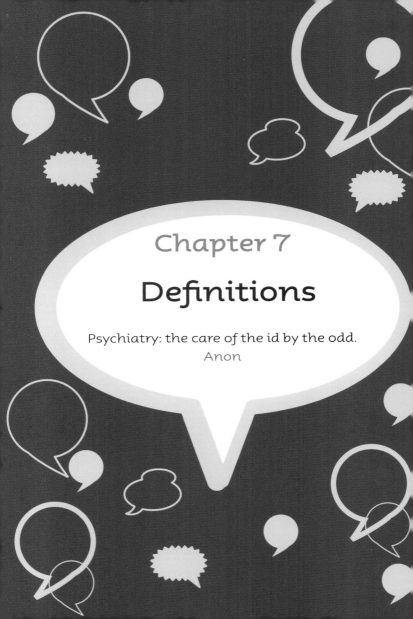

Chapter 7

Definitions

Psychiatry: the care of the id by the odd.

Anon

A selection of quotes which humorously explain the meaning of various common words.

• • • • •

Autobiography: An obituary in serial form
with the last instalment missing.
Quentin Crisp

• • • • •

Baby: A loud noise at one end and no sense
of responsibility at the other.
Ronald Knox

• • • • •

An alcoholic: A man you don't like
who drinks as much as you do.
Dylan Thomas

• • • • •

Preposition: An enormously versatile part of
grammar, as in "What made you pick this book
I didn't want to be read to out of up for?"
Winston Churchill

Book: What they make a movie out of for television.
Leonard Louis Levinson

· · · · ·

Cocktail party: A device for paying off obligations to people you don't want to invite to dinner.
Charles Merrill Smith, *Instant Status*, 1972

· · · · ·

Gossip: Hearing something you like about someone you don't.
Earl Wilson

· · · · ·

Redundancy: My definition of a redundancy is an air bag in a politician's car.
Larry Hagman

· · · · ·

Editor: One who sorts the wheat from the chaff and prints the chaff.
Adlai Stevenson

Happiness: Happiness isn't happiness unless
there's a violin-playing goat.
Julia Roberts

* * * * *

Journalism: A profession whose business
it is to explain to others what it personally
does not understand.
Lord Northcliffe

* * * * *

Censor: A man who knows more than he
thinks you ought to.
Laurence Peter

* * * * *

Gambling: The sure way of getting
nothing for something.
Wilson Mizner

* * * * *

Epitaph: An inscription which hopes that virtues
acquired by death will have a retroactive effect.
Ambrose Bierce

Egotist: A person more interested in himself than in me.

Ambrose Bierce, *The Devil's Dictionary*, 1911

• • • • •

Theology: The effort to explain the unknowable in terms of the not worth knowing.

H.L. Mencken

• • • • •

Cynic: A man who, when he smells flowers, looks around for a coffin.

H.L. Mencken

• • • • •

Revolution: An abrupt change in the form of misgovernment.

Ambrose Bierce

• • • • •

Education: The path from cocky ignorance to miserable uncertainty.

Mark Twain

Secret: What we tell everybody to tell nobody.
Ambrose Bierce

• • • • •

Kleptomaniac: A person who helps himself
because he can't help himself.
Henry Morgan

• • • • •

Success is getting what you want,
and happiness is wanting what you get.
Dave Gardner

• • • • •

Honeymoon: The morning after
the knot before.
Anon

• • • • •

Modesty: The gentle art of enhancing your
charm by pretending not to be aware of it.
Edgar Watson Howe,
Ventures in Common Sense, 1919

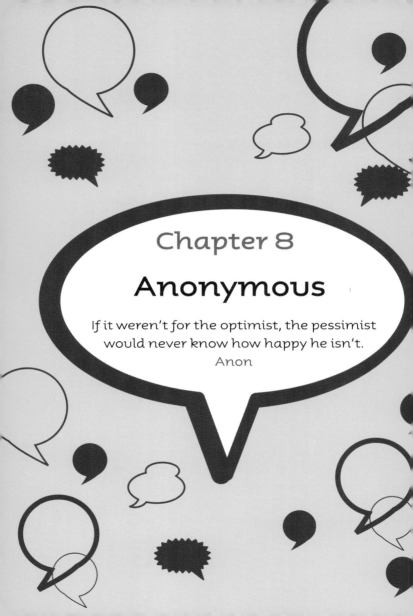

Chapter 8

Anonymous

If it weren't for the optimist, the pessimist would never know how happy he isn't.

Anon

It seems that some of the funniest words were said or written by A. Non. One wonders why he or she never owned up to them. And as well as off-the-wall humor, this chapter contains some excellent on-the-wall humor, a selection of graffiti culled from some of the world's finest rest rooms.

• • • • •

A groundless rumor often covers a lot of ground.

• • • • •

A gentleman is one who never swears at his wife while ladies are present.

• • • • •

I trust you completely, but please send cash.

• • • • •

Nostalgia isn't what it used to be.

• • • • •

A folk-singer is someone who sings through his nose by ear.

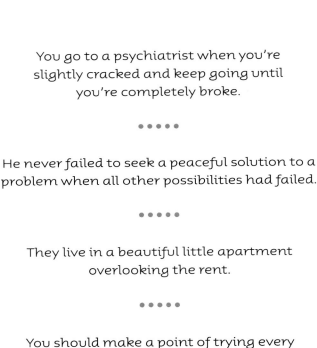

You go to a psychiatrist when you're slightly cracked and keep going until you're completely broke.

• • • • •

He never failed to seek a peaceful solution to a problem when all other possibilities had failed.

• • • • •

They live in a beautiful little apartment overlooking the rent.

• • • • •

You should make a point of trying every experience once, except incest and folk-dancing.

• • • • •

An after-dinner speech should be just like a lady's dress: long enough to cover the subject and short enough to be interesting.

• • • • •

Social tact is making your company feel at home, even though you wish they were.

Don't get annoyed if your neighbor plays his music at two o'clock in the morning. Call him at four and tell him how much you enjoyed it.

* * * * *

Modesty is the art of encouraging people to find out for themselves how wonderful you are.

* * * * *

A sadist is someone who refuses to be mean to a masochist.

* * * * *

People are very open-minded about new things as long as they're exactly like the old ones.

* * * * *

The wicked do well in this world, and saints do well in the next.

* * * * *

It is better to have an ugly wife for one's self than a beautiful wife for others.

An optimist will tell you the glass is half-full;
the pessimist, half-empty;
and the engineer will tell you the glass
is twice the size it needs to be.

• • • • •

Memory and teeth grow weaker with time.

• • • • •

I believe we should all pay our tax bill with a smile.
I tried—but they wanted cash.

• • • • •

Bigotry is being certain of something
you know nothing about.

• • • • •

Life is a hereditary disease.

• • • • •

Bad habits are like a comfortable bed,
easy to get into, but hard to get out of.

Better to get up late and be wide awake than to get up early and be asleep all day.

• • • • •

A: How's your insomnia?
B: Worse. I can't even sleep when it's time to get up.

• • • • •

Have your eyes ever been checked?
No, Doctor, they've always been blue.

• • • • •

Women tell everybody not to tell anybody.

• • • • •

A conscience is what hurts when all your other parts feel so good.

• • • • •

Two in every one people in this country are schizophrenic.

Chapter 9

Eating & Drinking

I always keep a supply of stimulant handy in case I see a snake—which I also keep handy.
W.C. Fields

A light-hearted assortment of remarks and puns about two much-discussed topics.

• • • • •

A gentleman never eats.
He breakfasts, he lunches,
he dines, but he never eats.
Anon

• • • • •

After four martinis, my husband turns
into a disgusting beast. And after the fifth,
I pass out altogether.
Anon

• • • • •

A psychologist once said that we know
little about the conscience except
that it is soluble in alcohol.
Thomas Blackburn

• • • • •

Love makes the world go round? Not at all.
Whisky makes it go round twice as fast.
Compton Mackenzie, *Whisky Galore*, 1947

The most sincere love of all is the love of food.
George Bernard Shaw

• • • • •

Let's get out of these wet clothes
and into a dry Martini.
Mae West

• • • • •

What, when drunk, one sees in other women,
one sees in Garbo sober.
Kenneth Tynan, *Curtains*, 1961

• • • • •

Sobriety is a real turn-on for me.
You can see what you're doing.
Peter O'Toole

• • • • •

Actually, it only takes one drink to get me
loaded. Trouble is, I can't remember if it's
the thirteenth or fourteenth.
George Burns

I always wake up at the crack of ice.
Joe E. Lewis

• • • • •

No matter what kind of diet you are on, you
can usually eat as much as you want of
anything you don't like.
Walter Slezak

• • • • •

My wife is a light eater; as soon as
it's light, she starts eating.
Henny Youngman

• • • • •

A man shouldn't fool with booze until he's fifty;
then he's a damn fool if he doesn't.
William Faulkner

• • • • •

Once, during Prohibition, I was forced to live for
days on nothing but food and water.
W.C. Fields

The worst thing about some men is that when they are not drunk they are sober.
William Butler Yeats

• • • • •

The best number for a dinner party is two—myself and a dam' good head waiter.
Nubar Gulbenkian

• • • • •

I will not eat oysters. I want my food dead—not sick, not wounded—dead.
Woody Allen

• • • • •

If this is coffee, please bring me some tea; but if this is tea, please bring me some coffee.
Abraham Lincoln

• • • • •

I went on a diet, swore off drinking and heavy eating, and in fourteen days I lost two weeks.
Joe E. Lewis

A fruit is a vegetable with looks and money.
Plus, if you let fruit rot, it turns into wine,
something Brussels sprouts never do.
P.J. O'Rourke, *The Bachelor Home Companion*,
1987

• • • • •

Artichoke: That vegetable of which one has more
at the finish than at the start of a dinner.
Lord Chesterfield

• • • • •

I'm on a seafood diet—I see food, I eat it.
Dolly Parton

• • • • •

You're not drunk if you can lie on the floor
without holding on.
Dean Martin

• • • • •

I'm not so think as you drunk I am.
John Squire

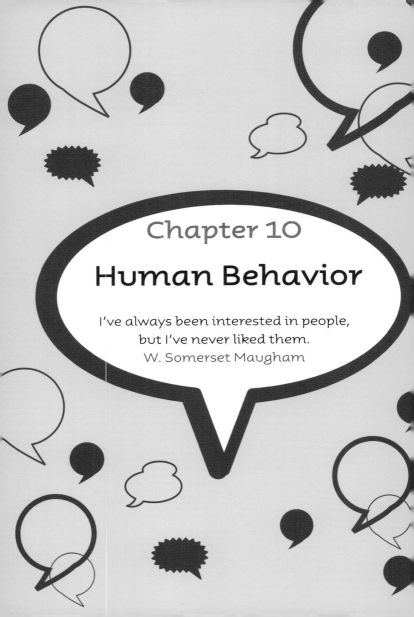

Chapter 10

Human Behavior

I've always been interested in people,
but I've never liked them.
W. Somerset Maugham

Does human behavior really change that much over time? The following observation was made by Lord Byron over 185 years ago, about a domestic servant abroad: "The perpetual lamentations after beef and beer, the stupid bigoted contempt for every thing foreign, and insurmountable incapacity of acquiring even a few words of any language, rendered him … an encumbrance."

• • • • •

I hate housework! You make the beds, you do the dishes—and six months later you have to start all over again.
Joan Rivers

• • • • •

If I have ever made any valuable discoveries, it has been owing more to patient attention than to any other talent.
Isaac Newton

• • • • •

To do each day two things one dislikes is a precept I have followed scrupulously: every day I have got up and I have gone to bed.
W. Somerset Maugham

Basic research is what I'm doing when I don't
know what I'm doing.
Werner von Braun

• • • • •

Even paranoids have real enemies.
Delmore Schwartz

• • • • •

I don't want any yes-men around me.
I want everybody to tell me the truth
even if it costs them their jobs!
Sam Goldwyn

• • • • •

Some people pay a compliment
as if they expected a receipt.
Frank McKinney Hubbard

• • • • •

I am extraordinarily patient,
provided I get my own way
in the end.
Margaret Thatcher

Why is it men are permitted to be obsessed
about their work, but women are only
permitted to be obsessed about men?
Barbra Streisand

• • • • •

Somebody's boring me, I think it's me.
Dylan Thomas

• • • • •

I can resist everything except temptation.
Oscar Wilde

• • • • •

When I'm good I'm very, very good,
but when I'm bad, I'm better.
Mae West

• • • • •

Actually, there is no way of making vomiting
courteous. You have to do the next best thing,
which is to vomit in such a way that the story
you tell about it later will be amusing.
P.J. O'Rourke, *Modern Manners*, 1984

To me, old age is always fifteen years
older than I am.
Bernard Baruch

• • • • •

I have noticed that the people who are late
are often so much jollier than the people
who have to wait for them.
E.V. Lucas, *365 Days and One More*, 1926

• • • • •

To Americans, English manners are far more
frightening than none at all.
Randall Jarrell

• • • • •

I like long walks, especially when they are taken
by people who annoy me.
Fred Allen

• • • • •

Forgive your enemies but never
forget their names.
John F. Kennedy

Punctuality is the virtue of the bored.
Evelyn Waugh

• • • • •

When a man tells me he's going to put all his
cards on the table, I always look up his sleeve.
Lord Hore-Belisha

• • • • •

I don't pay any attention to him.
I don't even ignore him.
Sam Goldwyn

• • • • •

No matter. The dead bird does not leave the nest.
Winston Churchill (on being told that his
fly was undone)

• • • • •

In my day, the principal concerns of university
students were sex, smoking dope, rioting, and
learning. Learning was something you did only
when the first three weren't available.
Bill Bryson, *The Lost Continent*, 1989

If one could only teach the English how to talk,
and the Irish how to listen, society here
would be quite civilized.
Oscar Wilde, *An Ideal Husband*,1895

• • • • •

If you think that education is expensive,
try ignorance.
Derek Bok

• • • • •

There are two kinds of failures:
those who thought and never did,
and those who did and never thought.
Laurence J. Peter

• • • • •

They say travel broadens the mind; but you
must have the mind.
G.K. Chesterton, *The Shadow of the Shark*, 1921

• • • • •

When choosing between two evils, I always like
to take the one I've never tried before.
Mae West

I do not object to people looking at their watches when I am speaking. But I strongly object when they start shaking them to make certain they are still going.
Lord Birkett

· · · · ·

Adam and Eve had many advantages, but the principal one was that they escaped teething.
Mark Twain

· · · · ·

Hollywood: A place where they shoot too many pictures and not enough actors.
Walter Winchell

· · · · ·

In examinations, those who do not wish to know ask questions of those who cannot tell.
Walter Raleigh, *Laughter from a Cloud*, 1923

· · · · ·

Life is what happens to you while you're busy making other plans.
John Lennon

I am a deeply superficial person.
Andy Warhol

• • • • •

For every person who wants to teach,
there are approximately thirty who
don't want to learn—much.
W.C. Sellar and R.J. Yeatman,
And Now All This, 1932

• • • • •

In England people actually try to be brilliant
at breakfast. That is so dreadful of them! Only
dull people are brilliant at breakfast.
Oscar Wilde, *An Ideal Husband*, 1895

• • • • •

France is the only country where the money falls
apart and you can't tear the toilet paper.
Billy Wilder

• • • • •

Poor Mexico, so far from God and so near
to the United States.
Porfirio Diaz

The brain is a wonderful organ; it starts working the moment you get up in the morning and does not stop until you get into the office.
Robert Frost

•••••

When in Turkey, do as the turkeys do.
Honoré de Balzac

•••••

Let's be frank, the Italians' technological contribution to humankind stopped with the pizza oven.
Bill Bryson, *Neither Here Nor There*, 1991

•••••

I could come back to America ... to die ... but never, never to live.
Henry James

•••••

In Boston they ask: "How much does he know?"
In New York: "How much is he worth?"
In Philadelphia: "Who were his parents?"
Mark Twain

Never criticize Americans. They have the best taste that money can buy.
Miles Kington

• • • • •

England is the most class-ridden country under the sun. It is a land of snobbery and privilege, ruled largely by the old and silly.
George Orwell, *The Lion and the Unicorn*, 1941

• • • • •

A person who knows how to laugh at himself will never cease to be amused.
Shirley Maclaine

• • • • •

What's on your mind?—if you'll forgive the overstatement.
Fred Allen

• • • • •

The English country gentleman galloping after a fox—the unspeakable in full pursuit of the uneatable.
Oscar Wilde

The English find ill-health not only interesting but
respectable and often experience death
in the effort to avoid making a fuss.
Pamela Frankau, *Pen to Paper*, 1961

• • • • •

I always thought that once you grew up you could
do anything you wanted—stay up all night or eat
icecream straight out of the container.
Bill Bryson

• • • • •

Americans are broad-minded people.
They'll accept the fact that a person can be an
alcoholic, a dope fiend, a wife beater, and even a
newspaperman, but if a man doesn't drive
there's something wrong with him.
Art Buchwald

• • • • •

It's the change of rhythm which I think
is what keeps me alive. In Spain I hear so much
noise from my window that I can't stand it.
In Switzerland it's the lack of noise
that drives me crazy.
Geraldine Chaplin

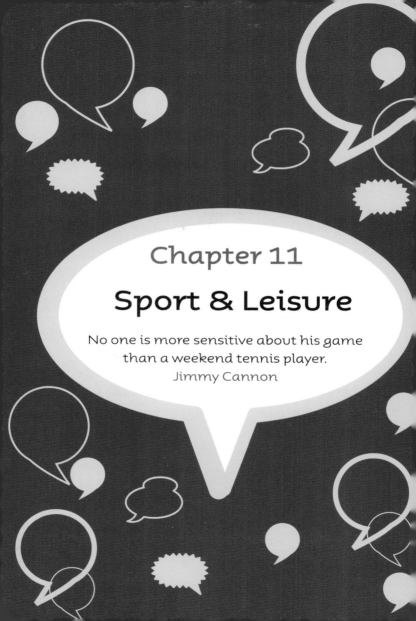

Chapter 11

Sport & Leisure

No one is more sensitive about his game
than a weekend tennis player.
Jimmy Cannon

A medley of entertaining quotations from the field of sport as well as some howlers made by TV and radio commentators, DJs, and politicians: the things they wish they'd never said.

• • • • •

Boxing's all about getting the job done as quickly as possible—whether it takes ten or fifteen or twenty rounds.
Frank Bruno

• • • • •

We didn't underestimate them. They were a lot better than we thought.
Bobby Robson (of Cameroon's soccer team)

• • • • •

Like a Volvo, Borg is rugged, has good after-sales service, and is very dull.
Clive James

• • • • •

Ever notice the older you get, the better athlete you used to be?
John Drybred

The least thing upset him on the links.
He missed short putts because of the uproar of
the butterflies in the adjoining meadows.
P.G. Wodehouse, *The Clicking of Cuthbert*, 1922

• • • • •

Golf is a good walk spoiled.
Mark Twain

• • • • •

The trouble with referees is that they just don't
care which side wins.
Tom Canterbury

• • • • •

Ten Tour de France riders crashed, two retired
after falls, another dropped out when diarrhoea
slowed him to the point of elimination ...
James Richardson

• • • • •

I don't exercise. If God wanted me to bend over,
he'd have put diamonds on the floor.
Joan Rivers

It's not only a race against the clock
but a race against time itself.
Presenter, BBC Wales

• • • • •

Years ago we discovered the exact point,
the dead center of middle age. It occurs when
you are too young to take up golf and
too old to rush up to the net.
Franklin P. Adams, *Nods and Becks*, 1944

• • • • •

If you want to take long walks, take long walks.
If you want to hit things with a stick, hit things
with a stick. But there's no excuse for combining
the two and putting the results on TV.
National Lampoon, 1979

• • • • •

The sport of skiing consists of wearing three
thousand dollars' worth of clothes and
equipment and driving two hundred miles
in the snow in order to stand around
at a bar and get drunk.
P.J. O'Rourke, *Modern Manners*, 1984

Everybody loves success, but they
hate successful people.
John McEnroe

• • • • •

If you watch a game, it's fun. If you play it, it's
recreation. If you work at it, it's golf.
Bob Hope

• • • • •

Leisure originally meant an opportunity to
do something. It has come to mean an
opportunity to do nothing.
Anon

• • • • •

Nick Faldo has shown himself to be a worthy
world number one by finishing second
here today.
Golf commentator

• • • • •

Sports do not build character. They reveal it.
Heywood Broun

A fishing rod is a stick with a hook at one end
and a fool at the other.
Samuel Johnson

• • • • •

It's quite clear that Virginia Wade is
thriving on the pressure now that the
pressure on her to do well is off.
Harry Carpenter

• • • • •

If you worried about falling off the bike,
you'd never get on.
Lance Armstrong

• • • • •

Playing polo is like trying to play golf
during an earthquake.
Sylvester Stallone

• • • • •

Whoever said, "It's not whether you win or lose
that counts," probably lost.
Martina Navratilova

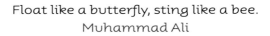

Float like a butterfly, sting like a bee.
Muhammad Ali

• • • • •

I'll let the racket do the talking.
John McEnroe

• • • • •

Most football teams are temperamental.
That's 90 percent temper and ten percent menta
Doug Plank

• • • • •

I am a winner. I just didn't win today.
Greg Norman

• • • • •

Ask not what your teammates can do for you.
Ask what you can do for your teammates.
Magic Johnson

• • • • •

No one knows what to say in the loser's locker room
Muhammad Ali

NOTES

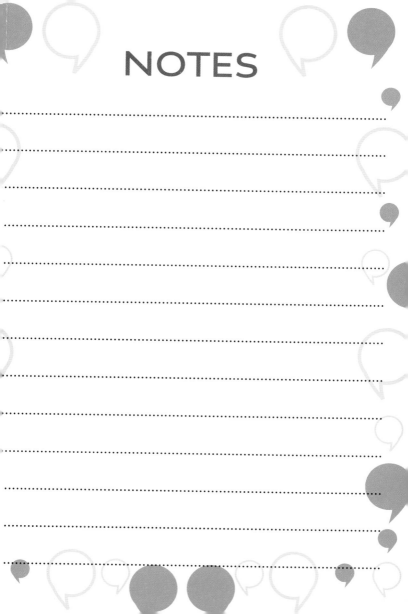

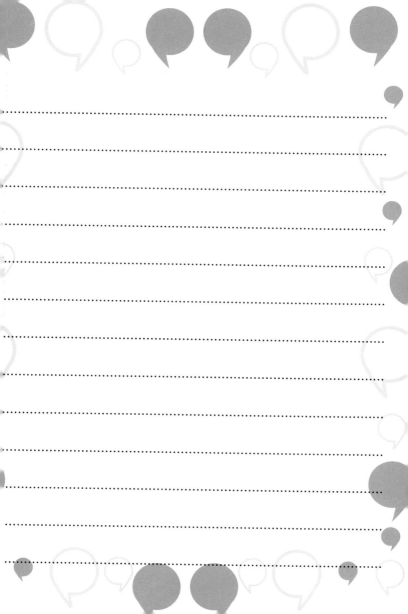

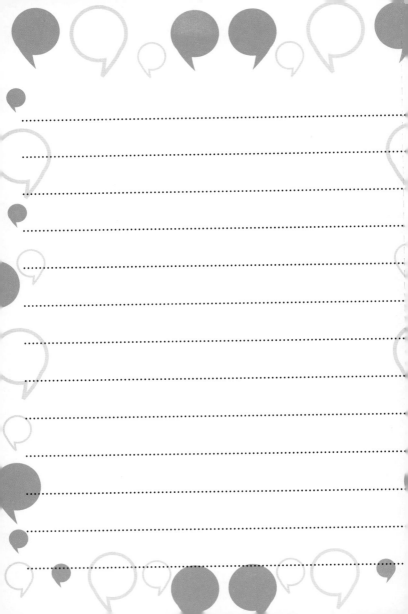

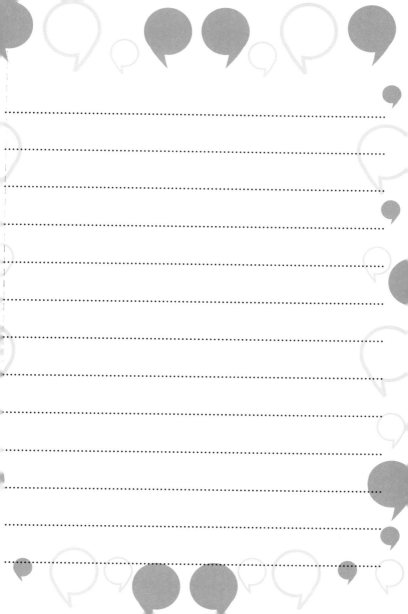

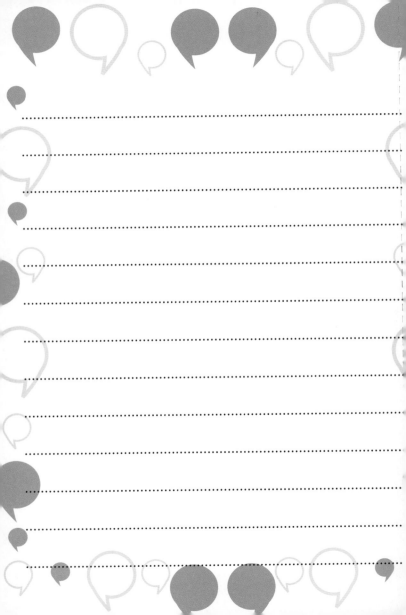

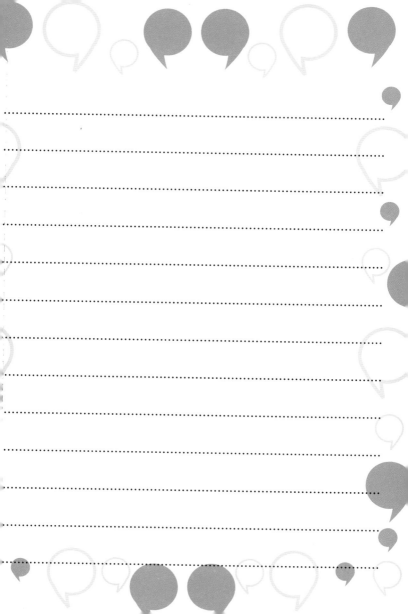

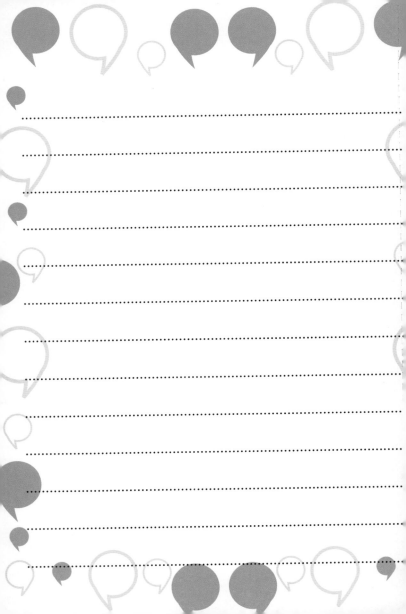

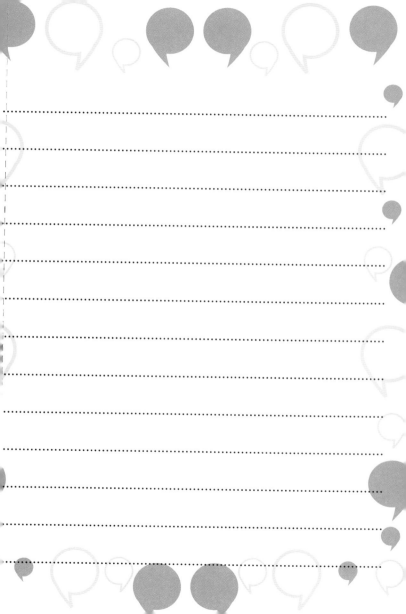

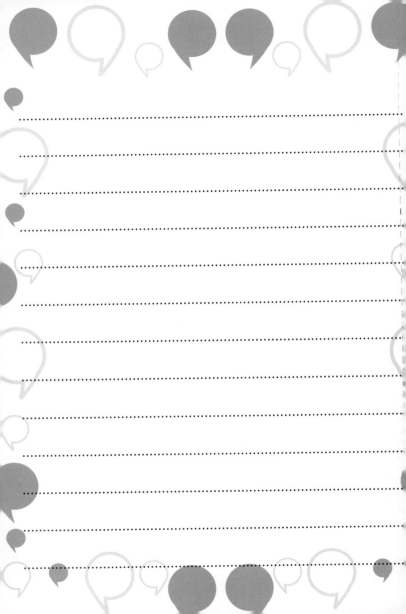

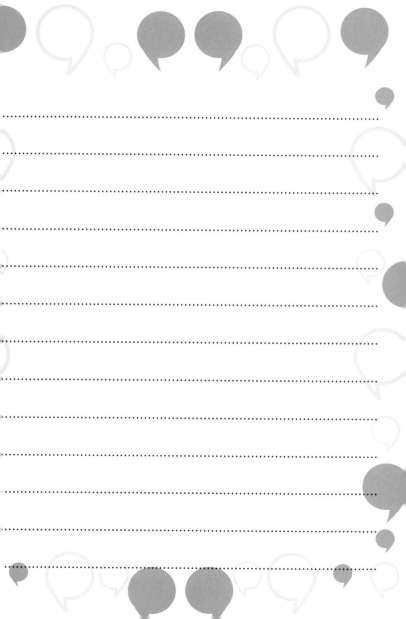

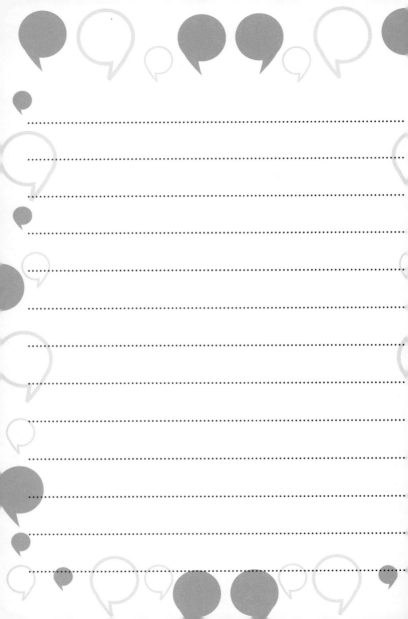

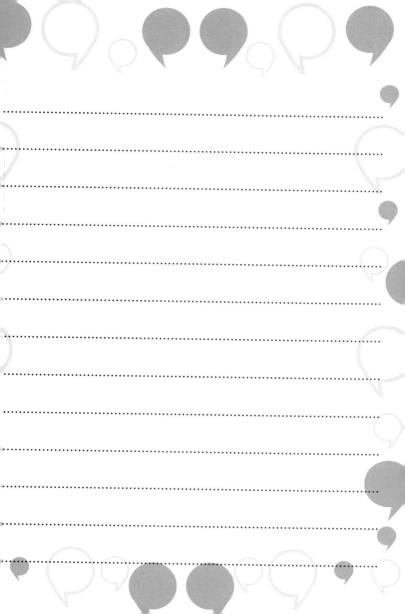

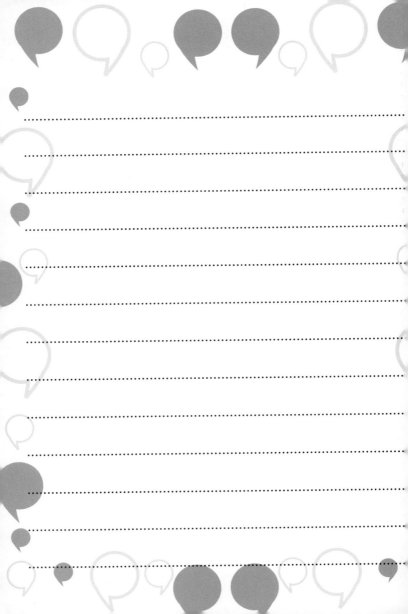

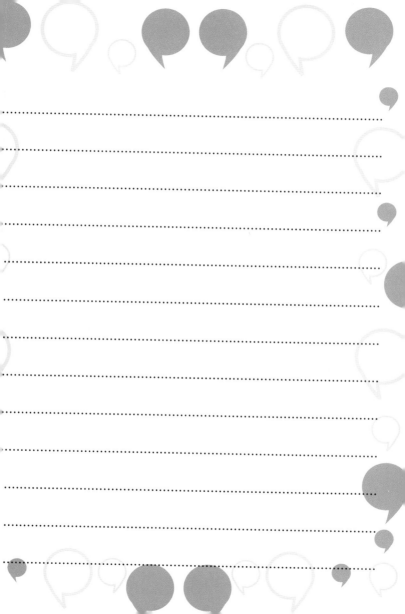

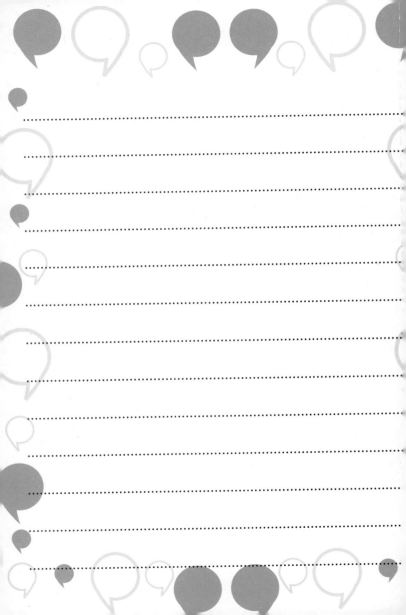